Bear, Coyote, Raven

by
Jason Grundstrom-Whitney

Resolute Bear Press
ROBBINSTON, ME

Resolute Bear Press, Robbinston 04671

Author Jason Grundstrom-Whitney wears many hats: poet, writer, songwriter, musician, lifelong activist, licensed social worker, substance abuse counselor, martial arts and meditation instructor, husband, father, grandfather, and a Bear Clan member of the Passamaquoddy tribe.

"Cedar, Sage, Sweetgrass" was previously published in *3 Nations Anthology: Native, Canadian & New England Writers*. "Ridin' Hard to Santa Fe" was published in the *Lewiston Sun Journal*.

Book design: Valerie Lawson

Printed on acid free FSC certified paper
by McNaughton & Gunn, United States of America

ISBN: 978-0-9988195-5-6

For Joan M. Dana

*Who taught me how to live in the world
and that our dreams and visions create our lives.*

CONTENTS

After Raven Stole the Light

Where Does He Go?

Rattles and Drums

Finding a Powwow

After Raven Stole the Light

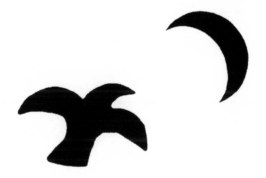

Ursa Major

Bear sat by the fire
with Coyote and Raven.

Looking up at the stars,
Coyote slyly asked Bear,
"How long do you reckon it would take
to get to one of them?"

Through the top of his head
Bear shot out,
leaving his furry clay body behind.
He became Ursa Major.

At times he played on the
stars in that constellation.
Around late-night fires
those beings wondered
about this sun and life.

He trailed purple as he sped in between,
listening for those in need of medicine.

"Good trip?" asked Coyote
as Bear shuddered.

Raven had stolen away;
the mist of dawn was calling.

Coyote

Walks along the trail
of the Milky Way.

Dust seeks dust;
wild seeks wild.

He hears the moon calling.
She is light years away,
leaving dust in his eyes.

Seeds of dreams
as light waxes
and wild wanes.

Doubt

Tired Raven stretched his wings,
his girth causing difficulty
on the downward stroke.

Too much pain—
his cold blue tears
created an ice storm.

A farmer shot at him.
An airplane almost
knocked him from the sky.

"How will I make it
to the top of the tree
before the day of renewal?"

Dragonfly

Bear ponders a dragonfly
landing lightly on his kayak.

"Am I not deserving your touch?"
Summer sleeps me lazily in this cocoon of plastic,
afraid to disrupt lilies and turtles from temporary
      perches.
My eyes lose most of what surrounds me—
insects, birds, frogs, jumping fish, menagerie clouds.

Your thousand-eye glance appears passive;
you alight from my kayak paddle,
seeing direction and winged prey in multitudes.

Dragonfly regards the world
with her compound eyes,
sees more of me than I know myself,
takes flight from the slipper of day
in late afternoon light.

Remember the Owl

"Watch the owl
in the woods at night.
How is it related
to the exhale of my breath?"
asked Bear.

"Watch the owl.
Listen to its call
You know its voice.
You see this area
in your dreams each night,"
answered Coyote.

"Watch the owl.
Listen. Remember."

Avian Bebop

Coyote tapped his foot
to the steady
walking bass line
of Charles Mingus.

"Yes, I like this.
It's like bedrock,
talking as it moves."

Coyote invited Raven and his kin
and anyone else who
would come.

After the concert
the sax player said
to the trumpet player,
"Damn, what happened
with our horns today?
They sang!"

They noticed the
crows and ravens
lining the telephone
wires.

Pebbles

We met in an arroyo
out past the neon lights,
Bear, Coyote, and Raven.

We ambled and ate
and gave crumbs to ants.

We took experience
like tiny pebbles in a rattle.

One pebble,
not very musical.

Put many in a gourd
and you have a conversation
through the night.

After Raven Stole the Light

1.

Eagle didn't bother Raven any more.
The old man was too tired to fight.
Raven stole the sun
the moon
the stars.

Eagle carried prayers.

2.

On a dark winter day
when the last gasp of a storm
whistled up the night sky,
Raven unleashed
light.

Through mischief and mystery
Spring was born.

3.

Raven, fat as night,
sat atop the world tree.

He shook his wings
to settle and roost.

Light shot from his feathers
spreading stars across
the blanket of night.

4.

Bear and Coyote
stumbled down the streets of Machias.

They were drunk, singing old songs
in a tongue not even the Tribes
could understand.

The earth smelled of musk
from seeds long forgotten
on Appaloosa fields.

The telephone wires
buzzed and hummed,
launching another refrain
as light spilled from the lip
of the ocean.
Raven flew with a broad smile.

Cedar, Sage, Sweetgrass, Tobacco

Coyote and Raven laughed
as my claws got caught up
in the fine strands of sweetgrass
I tried to braid.

"Unh," I swore,
forgetting my human voice.
I couldn't help myself;
the smell of the earth
and sweetgrass
brought out the claws.

Cedar, sage, sweetgrass, tobacco.

They found me in the blueberry fields
outside of Calais, Maine;
blue smacking lips
created a strange
contrapuntal line
to Raven's flight.

Coyote stole from the edge
of the field glancing cautiously.

Cedar, sage, sweetgrass, tobacco.

"Time for a trip."

"Unh, unh," smacked my lips.

Coyote looked west,
stood on two legs
and tucked his hair
underneath his hat.

Cedar, sage, sweetgrass, tobacco.

"What of the medicine?" I asked.

Said Raven, "We'll be back."

Warrior of Wide Open Spaces

If you travel vast distances
across the bones of burnt summer
remembering a place you saw
for a brief second thirty miles back,
how can you not be there?

If you happen to catch shadows
dancing in the wind,
you and they have been there,
impermanence the cadence
of a distant drum.

Don't mourn these places.
You find one another
in ten thousand years
in ten thousand ways.
You are and will be
the warrior of wide open spaces.

Edge of a Note

Moon-glow pearls cast the fields
and soak my jeans.
I dive into silver-frosted water
and swim underneath
to gaze up at the full moon.

In your distant howl
the edge of a note finds me
as I break the surface.

Wolf song reaches that part
I forget in the daylight
when the frenetic world
steals the edges of notes
and the howl fuels my heart
with an inaudible hum.

Mid-stride

You caught me mid-stride,
wild-eyed, confused.

You spoke through trees,
sun, stars,
rivers, mountains, lakes.

"Come home," you whispered
through the frosted grass.

You sang at night
through Ursa Major,
"Be who you are."

You caught me mid-stride
in a wild dash,
trying to put distance
from this clay body.

Wake Now

When I first came to your people,
you were scared, sick,
and did not know
the secrets of life's
abundant garden.

I married a woman and
taught her all I knew.
You are of that family.

Ignorance has a way
of tangling its diseased branches
tightly to the heart.
This happened many times.

Wake now, child,
and see, smell, taste,
feel silence and abundance
hidden within her robe.

Bear lifts his sleeping son
to greet the dawn.

Where Does He Go?

Horse Nation

Let me ride a wind horse bareback,
hold your long mane
in my fingertips and ride out
toward the great plains

past the crimson and gold of northeast forests
across granite ancient mountains
toward the sea of grass
collecting prayers from all beings

restless in the wind and feeling every grass blade
    on the great plains,
southwest across arroyos and canyons
wild nostrils intoxicated by mesquite, sage,
    and pinion pine

over young mountains with Indian paintbrush
    and osha root
blessing and collecting the prayer of bedrock
and beings dancing in the rich illumined air

to the Pacific Ocean
dipping under to the depths with myriad beings
    and their prayers,
sweet salinity filling blood and giving strength.

The horse and I run off a cliff in the northwest.
Heavily laden with prayers,
we run faster than light
to prance among the stars.

Heyoka Dancing

He saw the storm coming.
He took off his hat

and got on all fours.
He was above tree line.

Thunder beings
sang the air.

Lightning bolts
hit twenty feet away.

Bear dropped in a hollow
carved in rock.

He watched ancestors dance in light
as they zigzagged down to earth.

They burned and sang
in a voice beyond deafening.

Lightning struck
around the bowl where he lay.

Bear trembled and
felt the ground charge
with the ancestors' breath.

It was gone in minutes.
He rose off all fours and danced.

The wind smelled scarred.
His hair was wet with the oncoming rain.

TV, Powwows, and the New "Old Way"

Haven't heard him sing
'bout Indians,
coverin' everything,
everyone bein'
so correct
so polite.

Big powwow on TV.
Don't see no Indians.

Hey, didn't Columbus Day
go by with a whimper?

Nothin' like some powwows:
glitter, glamour,
enough food to feed Pine Ridge
for three months.

Turtle Island remembers
the compassionate footsteps
of the first Americans.

New "old way."
DON'T SEE NO INDIANS!

Where Does He Go?

They assumed he went to Florida.
On a particularly cold biting day
they predicted he would be gone.

Green frog skins lazily danced in the wind
and mingled with red and gold leaves
on the frosted wheat grass.

He walked slowly up the mountain.
Halfway he took off his hat and coat
and placed them neatly in a hole
in an ancient oak tree.

He stretched his paws on the cool forest floor.
He ate dirt and bark and binding material
that would enable a long rest without movement.
He tasted all life that has been or ever will be
in the dirt and smiled wearily.

The den smelled of aged fur and trapped breath.
He let himself feel into the space
and when ready, circled three times
and nestled into the soft silt.

He slept and dreamed constellations
that appeared in distant galaxies.
He watched beings come and go
and planets fall as their suns aged and died.

He walked across galaxies
in long wide strides
and offered what he could
of his generous medicine.

On a cool spring day
Stan saw him raking his lawn.
"Which part of Florida
do you go to?"

Bear smiled,
"Oh, the northern part."

Bear and Puma

"You gonna tell them or should I?" Bear stammered
gruffly.

"Well, you know it has to have meaning or it wouldn't be
a story told around campfires," Puma retorted slyly.

"Well, you didn't break my damn back, and you know
she didn't want either one of us. Raven nested with her
then flew off like he does," Bear said indignantly.

"Yeah, well, you know she is Pokoh's sister right?
She is all over mountain meadows this time of year.
She probably got tired of all our nonsense."

"So you gonna tell them or should I?"
They looked at a gathering of Ute
that welcomed Bear back from the mountains.

"Ah hell, let 'em have the story.
You know it didn't go down like that, right?"

Puma smiled and started to run up an old path.
"Haha," he laughed.

"Damn!" said Bear.

Raven's Flight

Raven whispered, "Love," into the wind.
All stopped and tilted their ears.

"Did you say that to me?"
Daffodil asked Dandelion.
"Yes, friend, but not this moment."

Deer looked at Porcupine,
no words just a tender glance.
Porcupine cooed.

Eagle flying high in the sky
normally took note
of mischief from Raven,
but she was caught talon to talon
with her lover.

They whispered in shrills
as they plummeted
in love's embrace.

Raven flew away
smiling.

Thunder Being

Bear heard their thoughts
were less than divine.

Buzzard hearing them
manifested malice.

Bear scooped some seeds
from his pouch and ate them.

Young roots grounded and
he became part of the clouds.

Wherever he saw or heard ignorance,
he stomped down shaking the very Earth.

When he passed on
and the rain swept the ground of being,
he shrank back to his earthly form.

Listening to thoughts
he shook his head in sadness.

"This used to work—
this used to work."

Dragon and Coyote

One day Coyote walks toward the east.
He sees a man stumbling
and right above him in the sky
this long colorful curious creature.

The man, hell, it's obvious he don't
know nothing's flying overhead.
Coyote decides
to cause some mischief.

He gets real close to that dragon,
only he don't know it's a dragon.
He ain't never seen one before.

He gets real close, and
they look each other in the eye.
The man don't know. He don't see nothing.

Well, I don't know who started it exactly,
but Coyote and Dragon just laugh and laugh,
and Coyote climbs aboard.

They look down at the man and laugh some more.
The man thinking he hears something, looks up,
and they laugh some more.

Just like that those two sail over the hills,
Coyote whooping as he rides Dragon's back.

That man stops, looks around, scratches his head,
then walks on with a puzzled look.

Tobacco Mingled with Prayer

The Milky Way slightly alters.
The dipper upturns.
The moon whispers softly
as I pray the directions.

Tobacco mingled with prayer
offered to the sacred fire.

Eagle Woman

1.

Eagle Woman sang with the wind,
her feathers melding with the air.

When the sun slipped lazily
into the blanket of night,
she landed on a beach,
her skin scented by rose.

2.

Eagle Woman rode across the desert
on an Appaloosa,
a single feather in her hair.

She found flight as the horse stopped
on the lip of a canyon
and her body transformed to
ride the wind toward the sun.

Her fierce eyes looked beyond material,
saw ghosts soar
beyond canyons, sage, and wind.

3.

Eagle dancers swirl and turn,
each step a flight beyond this moment.

On their backs I see prayers,
offerings for the morning sun.

4.

ka thum
ka thum

Eagle Woman rocked on her porch
smoking her corncob pipe.
Her great-granddaughter slept in a wooden cradle.

When she was young, the baby's mother
called her the original Wonder Woman
when she saw her come out of the forest
early one morning with a big doe
on her shoulders, tears
streaming down her face.

The night before the time of death
she gave tobacco and tears as offerings.

ka thum
ka thum

She wouldn't eat store meat.
There was no sense of the life taken.
There was no sense of the reciprocity of beings.
She would stay with her tears and tobacco.

ka thum
ka thum

She was tired and her shoulders ached
from the load of prayers and
flights to the dawn sun.
She knew there wouldn't be many more years
before the medicine was passed on.

ka thum
ka thum

Sometimes she thought about
that encounter with the Phoenix
and what he explained—
light, life, burn, ash,
passing onto the next rising.

ka thum
ka thum

She smiled as she thought of herself
as Wonder Woman and what spectacles
she had seen, her eyes
unaffected by the sun,
the tiniest flower and
towering mountains ribbed
across vast stretches.

ka thum
ka thum

Rain would soon come.
She could smell it bursting forth
from moss and pine.

She looked at the corn three inches high
and smiled,
"These young ones need rain."

ka thum
ka thum

She pulled on her corncob pipe.
There was nothing left but ash.

Death Stories

We made a fire
that night
and swapped
death stories.

It would seem a coyote
has many more lives
than a cat.

Raven?
"Hell, in some cultures he is…"

Wham-wham.

"Damn, there they go again.
This planet copulating
has got to stop.
Get a different galaxy,
would ya?"

Well, that led to
other conversations
not worthy of note.

Being Hungry

"Yeah, they tried to get rid of us.
They shot us, poisoned us,
   set up their dwellings out here."

The dog was curious and in awe.
"How do you eat? How do you
   live alone out here?"

"Well, you just eat when
   you are hungry;
   sometimes not.
You trust that whatever
   anyone throws at you
   you can survive.
Our customs and language
   have continued while being
   relentlessly pursued."
Coyotes are the Medicine People
   of the dog nation.

"Hmmm," mused the dog
   who had spent months
   learning the language.
"Thought there would be something
   deeper than this."

The coyote laughed
   as if reading his mind
   then disappeared behind a boulder.
Moments later he was
   an impossible distance
   behind another boulder laughing.
The dog nodded.

Medicine is not something
   that can be attained on a couch
   watching the history channel.
Sometimes you have
   to be hungry.

Silent Song

Alone, Coyote howls,
the moon awake,
the campfire
burned low.

Burning embers
embrace skeletal wood
like phoenix wings.

His prayer goes up
in a flag of steam
as the stars
sing silent songs.

Day and Night Flight

"And when the dawn breaks,
where do you rest your weary wings?"
asked Raven.

"There is nowhere to land.
All night I fly with no dreams to gather,"
said Owl.

"I am here now bringing in the dawn,
but you know I can't do that
until you have flown the night wind
and stitched the dreams of all beings
to this great web."

"There will be no sun today."
said Owl as she flew on.

Sawdust

It was time to hibernate.
I hitched back east
and walked the spine
of the Appalachians.

Raven circled above,
curious.
Coyote scurried among juniper
in the distance.

A bear is solitary,
the hermit of the wilds.

They knew I was pissed,
"Leave off. Can't you tell I am angry!"

Around developments we stole,
even high mountains leveled for mansions.

Raven circled.
Coyote scurried.
I left deep imprints in sawdust
at a new construction site.

Where to go
when there is nowhere to go?

Everyone's Sun

Late at night Coyote stirred the fire.
This didn't need to happen.
The world was burning.

Thick ash blanketed Bear and Raven.
The moon was quiet, a soft glow
highlighting snowflake ash.

Today the sun blinked
like a long Alaskan night.
Coyote stirred the fire.

There was nothing again to eat,
just the chants and tales
to keep frozen stomachs from cramping.

"Why do we immortals suffer time grown old
and watch everyone's sun
try to bring life to this charcoal world?"

Frozen Tears

Slumberous sun's
crimson light
kisses blue snow.

Warriors of flight,
chickadees,
dart through the cedars.

Koluskap's magic white canoe
and other impossible shapes
spread across the blue blanket.

Bear at the compost pile
stops in wonder;
frozen tears spill
on this morning's gift.

Coyote and Raven
watch quietly.

Thin Bears

Coyote saw an old man
run across a street in Quebec City.
He appeared young, but
on the other side
he stooped again.

"Found another," Coyote said
to Bear at an intersection.

Bear, Raven and Coyote
followed the man
to the back of a packing plant.

In the refrigerator room
they found two women and
the man Coyote had seen on the street.
They were very thin.

"What the hell are you folks doing down here?"
Coyote asked, taking off his hat
and letting the fur flow.

They changed to three thin white bears.

"We come down 35 years ago and
warned the tribes we were dying.
We could see the melt.
Now there is nowhere to hunt.
Countless of us have starved and died,
leaving bones for scrimshaw and medicine.
It is good to leave medicine,
but only in its place and time.
We are moving down."

Bear remembered his sister that died in 2002.
They found her emaciated remains on the edge
of a blueberry field near Calais, Maine.
Coyote and Raven sat with him and prayed
around the sacred fire for four days.

Bear felt death reaching in his new language—
drought, hurricanes, fire, auto-immune illness.
It seemed he added a new word daily.

"Our brothers and sisters warned others,
but the others did not listen."
Bear was angry as he thought of his sister
and the whales he had seen washed onshore
this past summer, their stomachs filled
with plastic.

The thin bears ate slowly so as not to get sick
from the hormone-fed sides of beef.
They stayed for a month until
strong enough to travel.

"There will be many more of us,"
said the old man.

Raven searched for new habitat.
Bear helped them walk.
Coyote encouraged them on.

Each time was getting harder
than the time before.

Sculpted from Silence

"Have you noticed that it is harder
to hear that hidden voice:
all day and all night,
planes in the sky,
cars on the greasy snake
and the collective sound," stated Bear.

"They hunt me more and
there are fewer places to go.
Ironic given the abundance of foods.
Just yesterday I was almost shot
lazing behind a dumpster after a fine meal,"
said Coyote.

"There is more jewelry,
but so few places to land safely,"
added Raven.

They heard from Owl, Deer, Badger,
Mouse, and many others
who had no solution at this exact moment.

In another meaningless meeting
a dreamer looked out the window
and slipped across vast terrain,
his teeth and claws growing longer
with each westward mile.

Bear Leaves Business

Bear was in the courtyard.
Overhead Raven squawked.
"Damn, Raven, can't you see
I am conducting business
with these suits?"

In the distance
beyond concrete
Bear smelled
the freeway.

"Squawk-squawk-squawk."

"But I really think this last piece of land...."
opined a suit.

Bear could only make out
the distance of the horizon
and his heart
spreading across the desert
away from sprinklers and cars
and fast-talking suits.

"Squawk-squawk-squawk."

Bear timed his step
past the last business meeting
he ever attended.

Bear's Night Watch

1.

Each grain of tobacco
Bear offers to the sacred fire
fills the air.
Prayer perfumed with scent
follows smoke and sparks
to the Creator.

He sits and holds space
for this family member
and looks on the trail of stars
and almost sees her flight
along the Milky Way home.

2.

His shadow casts across the field.
The trees in their silent watch
give him the strength and energy
to be awake.

He places another log on the fire
offering a prayer of thanks.

3.

The night grows cold.
Everything he is
is given in prayer
for her.

4.

Gray light.
The night watch is almost over.
Bear slowly rises and offers
another round of prayer.
Everything and all a circle:
fire,
prayer,
wind,
earth,
water,
stars.

All beginning
and coming home again,
never alone,
always changing,
always filled
with the great round
beyond what he thinks he knows,
but what he knows beyond thought
in the night watch
with the sacred fire.

‖ ‖ ‖

Dark Clipper

He moved in awkward eloquence
like a dark clipper
across the swamp.

Bear listened to the Moose Elder speak.
He talked with a tongue
as old as the forest.

"We have diseased livers and
we are weakened by ticks.
I am afraid this might be our last age.
We have no immunity for human greed,
depredation, and wanton destruction."

Bear pondered this and
felt the deep pain of Lyme in his joints,

"Let us move farther north," he opined.

The Moose slowly consented,
his long beard swaying in a slight warm breeze.

Smudge Sticks

The wild child within
weaves desert sage
high on a butte in New Mexico.

He sees a rainbow serpent
touching the mesquite far below.
He flies with a golden eagle
in the cloudless sky.

With bear paws
he digs osha root
in the mountain.

That wild one dies slowly in
concrete and glass, asphalt streets,
endless meetings,
and time schedules.

Away in fresh air
with sun on his face,
the wild child
weaves desert sage
into smudge sticks.

Singing Awake the Sun and the Moon

Coyote sang the moon awake,
and all beings glowed
with silver light and song.

Raven sang the sun awake,
and all beings glowed
with golden light and song.

Bear dreamed between the two,
and the universe was what it was
and shall be.

Rattles and Drums

Rock Bowl

Bear carried a drop of
the Atlantic Ocean in a tiny vial.

Raven had flown to the Northwest
and carried back a vial with
a single drop of the Pacific Ocean.

Coyote held a single dewdrop
from a Mountain Ball Cactus flower
from Bryce Canyon.

Three directions—this year it was Deer's turn
for the fourth. She brought a drop of water
from the Colorado River.

They met in northern Arizona,
now called the four corners,
and placed the drops in a rock bowl
they used each year.
Each added sacred medicines—
cedar, sage, sweetgrass,
and tobacco.

They stirred
medicine, water, and fine red earth
into the bowl.

Bear prayed.
It took longer each year
for this to work.
Water tables ran low.
The ocean cried in pollution.

After several days
rain fell again.

Bear, Coyote, Raven, and Deer
fell asleep near the rock bowl
and dreamed of golden tassels of corn
singing in the southeasterly breeze.

Flashflood

I am riding in a flashflood,
orange water
dashing through arroyos.

Raven and Coyote
laugh on the banks.

"Help, you idiots,
I am riding in a flash

f

l

o

o

d

!"

2.

Thrown out into the basin
like a cast in
bone games,

the ground
noisily nursed.

Bear was covered
in orange silt.

Coyote came,
followed by Raven
to see what had been left.

Fast food fortune?

3.

Bear shook thick orange
flakes of mud off his fur.

Raven dreamed of a sun burnt low,
refusing to edge the horizon.

Coyote sang to the moon
and in the space between notes
longed for days of abundance
and pawed an ant hill to stave off hunger.

Each orange flake fell to the ground
to become footsteps of future generations.

Bear decided not to drift into the night sky
and hang out with or be one of the dippers.

Coyote howled again pitifully.
Raven stirred and smiled
as his dream created a sustaining sun.

Bear made smudge sticks from desert sage
and let the smell create medicine
he would use tomorrow.

4.

The morning light
brought a carpet of cactus flowers
each framed
by the pregnant orange ground.

Prickly Pears

Coyote stopped to drink the mud water
of yesterday's rain.

Raven circled with jewelry around his neck
from a tin can he found on the black greasy snake
that bisects the freeway.

"Squawk-squawk," he bellowed
as cactus wrens clipped his flight pattern.
"They must be jealous."

Bear ambled below, stopped to eat prickly pears,
let the tiny thorns flush from his tongue
like thoughts of a different life
that seemed so long ago.

Cactus Flour

Coyote liked to be near the Tohono O'odham
when they harvested the fruit of the Saguaro.

These giants that gleaned crimson rays from sunrises
  and sunsets
had been home to cactus wrens that found solace in
  their thorns,
had survived brutal summers, and smiled blossoms in
  the spring rain.

Coyote watched Mawith gather her children.
They carried long poles made from the Saguaro spines.

She smiled as they went about their work.
At noon they ate meal cakes made with last year's flour
from the seeds of the giants.

"Careful now," she guided as one child's pole almost
  slipped
into a wren's nest.

She held a little child's hand as the older children made
their way back
to their homes with laden bags.

This night she showed them how to dry the fruit
and later how to grind the seeds with the slow
rhythmic pattern
like her reverent footsteps toward the giants at dawn.

Mourning Doves

Straining to hear their conversation,
a man fell from his perch
on the canyon wall.

Pierced by blood red stone,
his eyes blinded by the sun,
he listened fervently,
intoxicated by their love.

Well, you know how these things work.

Coyote and Raven pecked his skeleton clean.
Ants finished the job in their militant way.
Bones had nothing to hold them together.

He still listened,
intoxicated by their love
carried in sweet notes
on a wind
scented by pinion pine.

Mules on the Grand Canyon Rim

"Well, I guess the thing that bothers me is the
    asymmetry.
Fat white blobs atop our fine symmetrical muscle
hailing from places unimaginative.
Short names harsh as commands:
Iowa, Ohio.

White blobby offspring riding our fine backs,
looking like the wet circle on cones that drip on us
at the start of the journey."

"Can't we just throw them and run?" asked the
    novitiate.

The master smiled, "I had a dream once about
    open spaces,
running arroyos, the wind on my mane,
eating only what occurred to me."
Others gathered.
He talked like this through the night.

"If a child kicks one stone into another,
surely he will find a poet.
The universe seems to align itself so.
Walking steep canyon trails—
even a mule finds poetry."

Sacred Dogs

"I like to watch them when they run
and dance their sacred way
through arroyos and across desert sand.
Bolts of lightning flare
from their nostrils
and sleek muscles glisten with sweat.

Sacred dogs we called them.
We had not heard of horse.
Our experience was dogs
and though sacred
these dogs glided
through the narrow passage
between dream, vision, and reality."

Bear watched.

Raven clucked,
then wrestled the meat from the tendon
of a desert hare.

"Yeah, we remember," said Coyote.

In a rare moment of stillness
he sat down with Bear
to watch the ponies run.

Muddy Water

I look east at strange ghosts
dancing in the waves.
What mysteries could such dancers bring?

I wash in muddy water.

You lied and stole and wrote on leaves
with strange markings
about concepts we had never known.

With your smallpox and lightning sticks
ghost people danced red the soil
where now medicine is hidden.

I wash in impure water,
air holding lungs in a vise,
land barren and cold.

How can this skin of hers be so defiled?

Children play beyond this world,
beyond ghost sails and plague
sent to muddy water
and the dreams held so long ago.

Bear Dancers

Among the canyons and arroyos
dusty footprints wiped clean
as a sand painting after a healing.

Bear once sat in the circle as a human
and listened to Bear Dancers.
His blood marked the borders
of the four directions.

They walked, not saying a word,
ankle bells jingling with each step
shaking within him something
long ago forgotten—
like the smell of cedar in a campfire.

Song penetrated the silence,
the bells louder and louder
as they danced
on ponderous legs.

Sweat dripped from his brow,
gleamed drop by drop
like bluffs in the New Mexico light.

They danced, and he began
to feel fur and claws as the
slow rhythm became his heart.

Back in meetings,
dead concrete and windows
separated him from breath.
He tried to focus on words
beating into his soul.

It was then
the Bear Dancers taunted him:
glistening skin,
bells jingling,
his heart racing.

Everything opened
as he parted the veil
and stepped out
onto the desert floor.

Rattles and Drums

1.

Each pebble for the rattles
collected in reverence from an ant hill.
The hide stretched and
the wood seasoned to make a drum.

2.

Bear offered tobacco.
He invited the drum to sound and
held it next to his heart.

Raven and Coyote shook their rattles and danced
at times moving as human, at others swirling and
    twisting
in impossible shapes in fur and feather.

Bear started to see great beasts, brothers and sisters
    from long ago—
wooly mammoths, dinosaurs, tiny horses, and
    ancient men
hunting and making their offerings before the hunt.

He saw buffalo driven over cliffs,
and then the chase of sacred dogs
as men rode their backs and shot arrows.

He saw the ocean that filled this desert
and strange brothers and sisters
that swam the depths in countless lives.

He saw white sails and white men
that brought disease and
warfare and domination.

He saw men with six-guns
on Harleys
and priests hurt children.
He saw peacemakers—
sweat-lodges, sacred pipes, ceremony
and spirit plates that filled him and
his brothers and sisters with sustenance.

He saw every raindrop, river, stream, and ocean
and each drop disappearing—
then coming to be again in their bodies.

He saw dust from far galaxies collect and
formulate stars and planets and
the many lives he had known
across the trail of the ancestors.

He saw his relationship to each star,
each blade of grass,
each prayer,
each word spoken
in love,
in hatred,
in sadness,
in ecstasy.

3.

Dancing dogs, wolf, coyote
ran free from garbage dumps
and loud city noises,
collected in packs, mixed and full-blood,
played shadow with the sun.

4.

Raven calls.
Canyons fill and echo with possibility.
Rangers can't keep us from their caches.
They try everything.
We are not fooled
as humans gather more.

5.

Bear felt the medicine flow wide
then collapse
in taut circles around his heart.

Bear slowed the rhythm.
Coyote and Raven glistened with sweat,
their lungs burning, the far edges of their dance
trimmed to taut rings.

They left the canyon's southern rim—
Raven, to talk with a murder of crows
that had gossip from the Dakotas,
Coyote, to sing in the moonlight
across the border,
Bear, to talk with a white buffalo
in Wyoming.

Apache Tears

At the base of a cliff
women cried over
twenty-five warriors
driven to leap
by the U.S. Calvary.

They don't tell you
in history books
that those warriors
chose to leap,
soaring as eagles
with prayers from
and for their people.

They don't tell you
that women cried
and their tears
solidified into
black stones.

They don't tell you
about stories that
would make you
feel uncomfortable
as you walk
conquered land.

Bear remembered.
He could still hear
the women in the wind
at times
and held tightly
his Apache Tear.

Osha Root

1.

Bear could hear the annoying bells
of the hikers.

Raven had fallen in love again
and was nesting.

Bear was still mad at Coyote
who had offered to be
fire keeper for a sweat
he did with the Blackfeet.

No show.

Bear dug for osha root.
He smelled the pungent
camphor-like scent in the
aspen grove in Glacier.

He found the root and ate,
occasionally spitting on his fur
to keep the insects away.

It felt good to be at Glacier again,
to forget about bells sounding
and foul-smelling humans—

their tired streets,
their cruel self-righteous control—
using Earth as an ash tray.

He was content to be on all fours.

2.

At night Bear dreamed Ursa Major and Minor
into being and poured his generous medicine
to all in need.

3.

Bear heard and smelled the hunters.
They were not supposed to be here.

Their guns bellowed fire and killed a sister.
Young cubs wandered the forest crying.

4.

Bear came out of Glacier unwillingly.
Raven and Coyote harassed him
until he stood upright and
tucked hair under his hat.
"Unh, unh," he muttered.

"Ha ha ha," cackled Raven.
His long black hair in two braids
fell on his chest.

"Why now?" Bear stammered slowly,
his eyes wild and dreaming.

"Easy, big fella," whispered Coyote.

They always had to wait a while
when Bear went too far in.

Coyote and the Wee People

Long before the scent of
pinion pine and sage
filled the arroyos,
Coyote was there.

Long before the ice came
and scraped the land
to leave it emerald green,
the Wee People were there.

In the space between
words and laughter,
Coyote and the Wee People dwell.

They meet on vast plains of oceanic blue
to discuss the mischief it will take
to continue sending awareness
certain as whale song
to the stars.

Pickup Trucks and Coyote

You know Coyote.
When he came and saw this mess,
he thought he'd cause some mischief.

He changed alcohol to water,
public schools to learning centers,
cars to horses,
pollution to flowers,
power penises to pretty perennials,
hunger to abundance,
pain to laughter,
overpopulation to balance,
religion to children.
Everyone smiled.

You know what happened next.
Guns he couldn't change became
the gleam in the eyes of hunters
in the back of pickup trucks
shooting at the Trickster.

They shouted, "Where the hell
is that goddamn Coyote?"
The resounding report of rifle fire
stole his mischief.

Raven's Arrows

Raven was the best-looking
of the three.

Early in the morning
he flew deep into the desert.

In a canyon
with mesquite and sage
he found his cache
of shiny things.

He picked out
a golden necklace
found on the south rim
of the Grand Canyon.

Back he flew to L.A.

He swam in the air
above lovers.

He added his magic
to the good-hearted
yet shy males, afraid,
their stomachs twisted.

To the females he offered
eyes that saw only
perfection.

His golden necklace
beat against his strong chest.

Every lover caught
an arrow that night.

Raven flew back
to the canyon
satisfied.

Finding a Powwow

Finding a Powwow

1.

Coyote, Raven, and I
decided to go to a powwow
near Cheyenne.

We broke out our native
three-piece suits:
moccs, ribbon shirts
and jeans.

Our voices inhibited by dust,
we stopped for one beer.

Next thing I knew
there were three
Indians in lockup.

We missed the whole damn thing.
Who was gonna' bail
three Indians
even when they were wearing
three-piece suits.

2.

Coyote, Raven, and I
walked out of Cheyenne
and parted a while.

Raven hit the wind.
Coyote, "Well, who the hell
ever knew where that guy went?"

I stopped in a vast cornfield
to smoke some herb.
Couldn't find my way to the road.

Cars whizzed by,
my heart beating,
green corn tassels laughing.

I spent three hours
out there;
took a nap.

When I woke up, hell,
I was just in Nebraska.

Climbed the bank to where
fecund soil
met greasy tar.

Buffalo Blues

We climbed down
from the back of an 18-wheeler
on the edge of the Great Plains.

A freak Alberta Clipper
had dumped six inches of snow.
The warm sun made the plains
look like an Appaloosa,
snow and June grass.

I played my harmonica,
each note lost in
the vastness of grass
and snow and sky.

Raven flew.
Coyote foraged.

I played blues
about this horse nation,
the Buffalo Calf Woman,
and the times I could talk to people
and they understood
and how it felt to be so alone now,
each note evaporating as I played
like the Appaloosa fields.

A horse trailer stopped next to me.
They led a colt out.
He took in the air and danced.
Coyote paused to listen.
Raven circled above.
I played on and on.

The Continuous Buffet

1.

An interesting notion
hit Coyote.
"Suppose I just wait
by a dumpster? That way
I won't have to do this
endless searching. It will be
a continuous buffet."

Raven looked at Coyote slyly,
"Sure, why not give it a shot?"

That day Coyote ate
like a king.

Fatigued by gluttony,
he lay behind the dumpster.
"This way I shall never be
caught," he thought.

In the early morning
a loud monster came and
swallowed Coyote's kingly
feast in one gulp.

On top of this insult
it set the dumpster on his tail.

Raven laughed all morning long.

2.

It took Raven three days
to find me; my paws were
elbow deep in a hollow trunk,
my lips smacking honey.

"Oh, all right," I said
retracting golden-hued claws

We hitched back to L.A.
in two rides. The last one was
with a guy named Lucky
who hawked stuff at
gas stations for fuel.

We drank sangria, smoked
fat cheap cigars, and told
urban legends. Lucky dropped us
off in Watts at 3 a.m.
I played harmonica.
Raven worked the crowd.

We needed money
for Coyote's broken tail.

3.

There was that dumb shit
slunk behind the dumpster
sobbing.

Bear picked up that green
rusty box with one paw.

Coyote took off fast,
howling down the alleyway.

It didn't take long to hit desert,
less time still to hide
and whimper where
no one could hear
except maybe lizards
and such that have
their own kind of laughter.

4.

I awoke with a start,
the cold desert night
filled with stars and
black sketches of
jagged mountains.

Coyote howled
in a distant canyon.

Raven was buried
in an old ratty
sleeping bag,
his hair the night
against iridescent skin.

Something was stuck in my eye.
I fell back to sleep
and dreamed of digging osha root.
Dust kicked up
and collected other dust
becoming stars and constellations.

Four Directions in Steel

Bear lay in the bottom of a dumpster
four directions in steel
looking up at the stars
in the dark dome of night.

"How very far,
how very near
I am.

"If I lose everything,
there is everything
to gain.

"Life's path is not vertical.
It is the roundness of a circle,
in the middle, nothing."

Bear lay at the bottom of a dumpster
his hands resting on his full belly
so very near
so very far.

Desert Tortoise

Coyote pawed the desert tortoise
near a wound on the back of her shell.

The tortoise pulled in her head.

Raven flew above, listening for death.

"Leave her be," scolded Bear.

"My sister, that looks like it was a horrible battle
you had; how long ago?"

Her head reappeared.
"What year is this?" she asked.

They figured she had been shot with musket fire
in the 1600's.

"I gave an eloquent speech that day,
summing up all I had learned from the desert
as they kicked me and shot me and left me for dead."

"Impossible," muttered Coyote, "why that is …"
His tongue hung out as he did math in the air.
"Let's see, carry the one, well, a long time!"

"What have you learned since?" asked Bear.

"Patience, my child, patience."

Raven flew on for better pickings.

Coyote, Bear, and Concrete

Coyote drifts along trails scented with
pinion pine and mesquite.

He looks at Bear.
They laugh.

Caught in this broken down world
there ain't nothing that can bring
these wild freeway eyes
onto the blank cold stare
of concrete and asphalt.

Coyote and Bear drift
among the pinion pine and mesquite.

Ridin' Hard to Santa Fe

1.

Tucked my hair
under my hat.
Tiny particles of sand, sage
and tumbleweed
blasted my face.

Storm coming.
Pulled on my overcoat,
head bent.

Stepping from vision
had always been
hard for me.

Ahead the glow of
city lights.

2.

Felt tar underneath my feet,
the give of sand,
soil abruptly ending.

Greasy hardness
penetrating bone.

They said there wasn't much
to eat in the mountains
that winter.
Town officials gave the go-ahead
to shoot bears
feeding in dumpsters.

Out back of Santa Fe
rich folks were trying
to lop off mountaintops
for views and such.

I shook my head,
hair fell,
coat unraveled.
I heard the click-clack
of my extending claws
on the hard road.

3.

Let them shoot me.

Saw a family in a
dumpster once.
Best act of fatherhood
I ever saw.

Kind gentle eyes
feeding his family.
Nothing for himself.

When discovered,
he was chased and beaten
as his family ran to safety.
St. Survival I called him.

Hell, they even chase
their own kind
from dumpsters.
Might as well tempt fate.

I jumped into the rusted
steel container.
Let them shoot.
I smacked loudly
on day-old honey-glazed
doughnuts.

4.

An old man approached,
my thoughts then of earth
and roots
and healing.

The old man laughed.
I laughed.
I climbed out of the dumpster
and we walked
the road to the desert.

That night we smoked
and sweated
and told stories,
his tribe,
my tribe,

and we remembered
a time when we walked together
for a short while.

5.

Tucked my hair
under my hat.
Could taste tobacco
and frybread.

Fur and claws
retracted,
I walked by
his kitchen window.

We stopped to look
at one another,
my ponderous steps
slowly transitioned.

Stomping,
I laughed.

There was a helluva
thunderstorm that day
outside of Santa Fe.

Counting Coup in Pecos Wilderness

Coyote pawed the ground
and looked to the south.

Raven flew in ever-widening circles
toward the north.

"Ungghh," intoned Bear.

They could not understand
the silence Bear needed.

They left him on a mountaintop
in the Pecos Wilderness
in a thick grove of ponderosa pine.

Coyote made it to Mexico.
He was almost shot three times near Las Cruces
before slipping across the border.
He sang of lost love
on a porch with a Tarahumara family.

Raven swam the sky
and made his way to the Haisla
to create mischief.

Bear set his old jeans and torn tee-shirt,
neatly folded, on a flat rock
like an offering.

He set his gaze on the
desert floor far below.

He sat through late afternoon
as Hare nudged him and laughed,
looking back at his brothers and sisters.
Bear smiled at this counting of coup.

Through the night
he looked into the
space between stars.

At 6:45 a.m. the U.S. Air Force
flew in formation
back and forth for two hours.

In the afternoon a hiker
found paw prints
in the soft red earth.

Rt. 9, Hidalgo County, New Mexico

Each note gets lost in vast space.
I swear I see a cloud dance
to the melody of my harmonica
and the tumbleweeds
move to the rhythm.

No one here for miles
but the bleached bones
of cattle and deer
hit long ago.

Back east they dream of building
and dancing to the tick-tock
they presume to be indelible time.

Out here the hot whisper of mountain air
scented with desert sage
blows away any notion
of kept moments.

Up ahead wild horses run across the road,
long hair flowing north,
noses pointed to the Animas Mountains.

I step closer, each step faster
until shoes give way to feet,
feet to hooves, my nose attuned
to the smell of sweat, sage, and pinion.

Back east in a meeting
surrounded by steel, concrete, and glass,
I pull a Barrel Cactus spine
from the sleeve of my suit.

Walkin' to Reno

Coyote, Raven, and I
bent into the wind
and walked toward the city.

It's a curious thing
about vagabonds
and their coats.
They hold insects, mesquite,
tiny fingers of tumbleweeds.

We found the city street,
desert abruptly meeting
asphalt.

It was not long before
we were drunk
to the sound of buzzing,
snapping electrical wires.

We sang with
coarse-sanded throats,
melody resounding
and ending abruptly
where the tar met the sand.

Everyone's a Critic

They found an old guitar
in a dump outside Santa Fe.
"I knew this once,"
said Bear.

He picked up the guitar
and immediately broke all the strings
with his claws.
"SHIT!"

Coyote pounded on
old discarded tins
of peaches and pears.

Raven laughed at Bear
and sang an old song he had learned
in crow-ese.

"Dammit, Ethel," muttered Ernest
trying to sleep in his house by the dump.
"What the hell is that infernal racket?"

Gateway

They were tired
after getting a ride
through the night
from a long-haul trucker.

St. Louis,
gateway to the west,
'cept they were headin' east.

Raven complained about
tuckin' his hair.
Coyote nudged him,
"Just do it already."

Bear heard a woman's voice.
She was a street preacher
dressed in ragged clothes
and her long hair had
ribbons of every color tied in.
Her face was deeply lined
like the Black Hills.

"The world has a chance, but your choices
need to reflect the future and not selfish greed.
Long has this sacred skin carried you,
nurtured you, sustained you, kept you aloft
in the cosmos as we plummet
through space."

"C'mon, Bear, let's go.
She is just a street preacher.
We have heard tons of 'em,"
said Coyote impatiently.

"Look," said Raven, "BB King tonight,"
pointing at a poster on a telephone pole.

Raven and Coyote grabbed Bear
by his blue coat,
and before he knew it
they were in the concert hall.

Bear watched as Raven and Coyote
worked the crowd.
He thought of a burning world.
That preacher he knew was Mother
manifested on a dusty street
of the gateway to the west.

How Do You Dress a Medicine Man?

In brightly colored beads
made at sweat shops
you parade him around powwows
like a peacock?

Should we apologize
to every Elder?
"Why, what did you do, my friend?"
they might ask with bright winking eyes.

Should we pay for sweats
and kiss the feet of someone
who seems to know songs
and dances in all the right places?

I ask you, "Have you found the lesson
of an ant in the Arizona sun?
Have you drifted with a Golden Eagle
lazily over canyons?
Have you talked to trees
and gleaned a whisper in their
gnarled tongue which rings
sweeter than our guttural
note-globs?
Have you sat in meditation
for an entire day
just to hear your own heart?
Have you listened to corn tassels
singing in a slight breeze?

How do you dress your medicine man?"

When We Surrender

Raven flew across vast oceans
and continents
gathering all that obscures.

The flight was heavy;
the load immense:
greed,
envy,
lust,
hatred.

Raven never complained.
What was surrendered
could be absorbed.

A great alchemist,
Raven burned chaff into light
spread throughout the new year.

When Bear Tells a Story

Bear leaned back against
the cold frame of the wigwam.

He took in a deep breath
and began to tell stories
as the fire cast shadows.

Bear talked all winter.

Raven and Coyote
circled the camp,
causing mischief and
at times assumed human form
to listen.

I still hear him
across the cold blue
as I snowshoe,
each step on the unblemished foolscap
a remembrance for what was
and what will be.

Author Biography

Jason Grundstrom-Whitney is a poet, writer, songwriter, and musician. His poetry has been featured recently in *3 Nations Anthology: Native, Canadian & New England Writers* and the Underground Writers Association's *Anthology of Maine Poets. Bear, Coyote, Raven* is his first book of poetry.

Jason is a lifelong activist working for Native American rights, Sexual Assault and Domestic Violence survivors, Hospice and end of life, homelessness, the environment and climate change, and bringing alternative medicine to allopathic medical thought. A University of Southern Maine graduate and an LADC/LSW, Grundstrom-Whitney works as a Substance Abuse Counselor/Co-occurring Specialist at Riverview Psychiatric Hospital in Augusta. Past positions have included hospice social worker, school student assistance counselor, and Tai Chi, Qi Gong, Bagua, Xing Yi Quan, and meditation instructor.

Jason has studied with Thich Nhat Hanh, Joan Halifax, Ken Cohen, Shou-Yu Liang, Al Gardner, his Clan Mother Joan Dana, as well as his sister Brenda Lozada and numerous other Native Elders. He has been in recovery for 37 years and writes from his experiences hitchhiking around the U.S. for two and a half years and learning from the many everyday masters across cultures he has met in his travels.

Jason is a husband, father, grandfather, and a Bear Clan member of the Passamaquoddy tribe.